The People in Your Life Are a Gift

DR. LARRY STANLEIGH

Second Edition

ABOUT THE COVER

Pratibha Tina Gohill, circa 1965, Nakuru Kenya

© 2023 Dr. Larry Stanleigh and L. Stanleigh Prof. Corp.

Published by: L. Stanleigh Prof. Corp.
Edited by: Denise Summers, Amphora Communications
Designed by: Cecilia Humphrey, Creative Capture

ISBN: 978-1-7780202-3-0 e-book
       978-1-7780202-2-3 print

All rights reserved.

No part of this publication may be reproduced, stored in retrieval system, or transmitted in any form by any means (electronic, mechanical, photocopy, recording or otherwise) without prior written permission of Dr. Larry Stanleigh and the L. Stanleigh Prof. Corp.

Lawrence M. Stanleigh
BSc, MSc, DDS, CIME, FAGD, FADI, FICD, FACD, FPFA
Calgary, Alberta, Canada

www.drlarryspeaks.com

Dedicated to
Tina, Isabel and Samara
Three of the greatest gifts
a man could ever wish for

Prologue

It's 2001. I am in Boston for my very first American Academy of Cosmetic Dentistry (AACD) convention. It is the largest such convention I have ever been to with over 5000 dentists and dental team members attending.

At most conventions they often start their days with a keynote speaker and on the first day of this convention, they start each day like this too.

I am sitting in a large auditorium with 5000 people. They turn out the lights, a spotlight fills the center of the empty stage, and from the side rolls a motorized wheelchair into the middle of the stage. It is clear this man is disfigured, and is a quadriplegic. He has a commanding voice and tells a powerful story.

His name is W. Mitchell and he tells the incredible story of how he was first injured in a horrific motorcycle accident, followed years later by a plane crash. For the next hour, he has the entire room silent as he weaves storytelling into his message. His is a powerful message of improbable survival and resilience, and the determination to not accept defeat. Without props or pictures, through the power of his voice alone, he impacts us all. The lights come up, and everyone moves off to the various other lectures and courses they want to attend.

Not a single person leaves the auditorium the same as when they entered. I sit there and say to myself, "WOW! One day I want to do that."

This book is the written form of a keynote address that I now deliver. A story of deep emotion, of love, and of gratitude. I hope you enjoy reading it. May it impact you in surprising ways.

1
Nakuru, Kenya

She was born in the garage of the family home in Nakuru, Kenya, the third child of what eventually will be six children to Kanti and Kamla Gohill. Her grandparents had moved to Kenya from Gujurat, India when they were young to help the Brits build their brick homes and the railroads in East Africa.

In traditional Hindu Gujarati households, the aunt, who is the father's sister (called foi or phoi) is given the honour of naming the children and she gave this newborn girl the name Poonam (which means Full Moon). The family was delighted with her choice. The grandfather walked into town a few days later to register the birth with the authorities and came home with an official birth certificate. He had given the baby the name Pratibha (which means Intelligence, Splendour, and Brightness). The aunt was incensed. How dare he take away her right to have named this child! In protest, she refused to call the girl Pratibha at all. In fact, she would not even use an Indian name and chose an English one instead, just to annoy her family. She called her Tina. And Tina is how she has been known ever since.

2
Calgary, Canada

Years passed and with a family of six children, Tina's mother was worried about the future of her sons and daughters. The oldest son wanted to be a doctor, and in the tradition of their culture, he would get his wish. But he would have to travel to another country, another continent, to be educated in medicine and would likely never return. The daughters would be paired off in arranged marriages, with substantial dowries required, moving away to become the property of their husbands' families, quite possibly back to India or somewhere else. After spending money on their oldest son and the two dowries, there would be little money left. The remaining three sons would not get the educational opportunities they deserved and would have to find their own way. Kanti's oldest brother had become a doctor, was educated in England and had moved to Canada.

Kamla encouraged her husband to follow this brother to Calgary, Alberta, Canada, and off they went. At the age of thirteen, Tina left the life she had known at the equator in Africa to land in Calgary in mid-January to -17C temperatures and snow.

Tina graduated from high school at sixteen, studied food science, then worked in retail in the jewelry business. She finally became an optician at the North Hill Shopping Mall in Calgary.

One day, on a work break, she walked to the mall's food court, to a concession called Mmmarvelous Mmmuffins. She lined up behind a friendly, balding fellow who was joking with the girl at the counter. He gathered his things, turned around, flashed a big smile, and left.

Tina remarked to the girl behind the counter that she thought this guy was funny, and cute too.

The girl said, "Yes, he is like that all of the time, and you really think he's cute?"

Tina replied, "Yes, and if you know he is like that all the time, he must work in the mall...Do you know where he works?"

She replied, "No, but I'll find out."

The next day, he showed up to get a muffin and hot chocolate and the girl behind the counter informed him that someone in the mall thought he was cute. He laughed it off and went on his way. This fellow was a creature of habit, and every day he returned to have his muffin and hot drink, and every day she told him the same thing, that there was someone in the mall who thought he was cute.

Finally, he said, "It does not do me any good to know someone thinks I am cute if I don't know who it is."

To which the girl replied, "Give me your phone number and maybe she'll call you."

He wrote his number on the back of his business card and gave it to her, but he suspected it was the girl herself. She was only sixteen, he was in his 30s, and was not interested in her.

Later that same day, Tina arrived at the muffin shop and the girl handed her his business card. Now the pressure was on. It was not common for women of South Asian origin to be cold-calling a man to ask him out (this was the early 1990s, as well). Tina was reluctant and afraid to call. What if he did not feel the same way? What if he rejected her? Her co-worker, who had also met his girlfriend in the mall, told her she had nothing to lose. And after two weeks, she gathered up the courage to call him.

———

It was Wednesday night, 7:00 PM. The telephone rang and I answered it, "Hello?"

"Hello, this is Tina from the mall."

As you may have guessed by now, I was the friendly, balding guy who bought muffins every day in the mall.

I immediately knew who this was. It was the woman who said she thought I was cute, and I never get told that, so I decided that I am going to give this woman my time. We talked for over two hours. Here I was, a white Jewish fellow of North Eastern European origins and she, a brown, East Indian Hindu woman from Africa. Nevertheless, we shared a lot of common values...family, culture, interests, food, movies and more. I had no idea what Tina looked like, but I had to meet her.

The next day, I walked over to the optical store to meet her. She was in a pink business suit (jacket and skirt), white blouse with black-rimmed glasses and had a nervous smile. I smiled in return and off we went to have

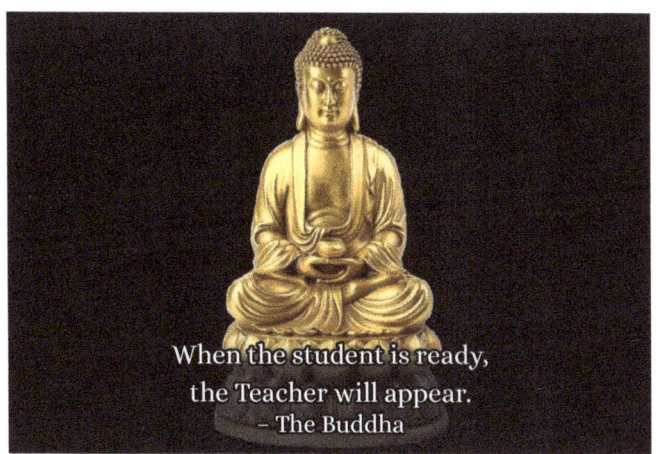

a break and get to know one another. The girl behind the muffin counter was surprised and delighted to see us together.

You know the expression, "When the student is ready, the teacher appears."

I paraphrase that as "When the person is ready, their partner appears."

We were ready. One year later, we were engaged and the next year married. The wedding weekend was an amazing four-day affair...but that is another story.

3
Colour Blind

It is one year after our marriage. Tina is in the first trimester of pregnancy with our first child. And we have decided to go on a trip of a lifetime. We travel to Bali, the only place on Earth that is predominantly Hindu, outside of India. Its form of Hinduism is very ancient as the country had been isolated from India for centuries.

It is truly a magical place. We loved being there. Bali is a volcanic island with significant rainfall and fertile soil, surrounded by an ocean with abundant seafood. The people who live there do not have to work hard to feed themselves. They have a lot of free time and they devote themselves to the arts and artistic expression of their faith. Each village seemed to have a different specialty in art...oil paintings, wood carvings, cloth weaving, dance, theatre...it was beautiful.

We started in the centre of the island in Ubud and then moved to Nusa Dua where all the big hotels were. Each night we dined in a different restaurant. A couple of foodies, we were in heaven. One of our meals was in Nampu, the Japanese restaurant in the Grand Hyatt Hotel. Labour Day had come and gone and the mostly white tourists from Australia, New Zealand and Europe had all left. I was looking around the restaurant and saw that everyone else in the restaurant was either Balinese or South East Asian.

So I leaned towards my lovely brown wife and said to her, "Do you realize that we are probably the only two white people in this restaurant!"

To which she lovingly replied, "Look again."

I am truly colour blind.

4
Foothills Hospital

It was March 20, 1996. The weather was cold, blowing snow, blustery and unpleasant. Tina was eight days overdue, pregnant with our first child. Labour had finally started. Off to the hospital we went, only to learn after about six hours she was not dilating more than one to two centimetres and we were sent home.

After two additional exhausting days of labour, I was worried that I wouldn't be able to drive us back to the hospital safely. So off we went, again. Now we were back at the hospital, hoping for this baby to finally appear. Tina had been given a spinal anaesthesia to assist her pain management. She had dilated more, and in the pause between contractions, we both fell asleep. When the obstetrician came in and checked on the mom and baby, he observed that with each contraction, the baby

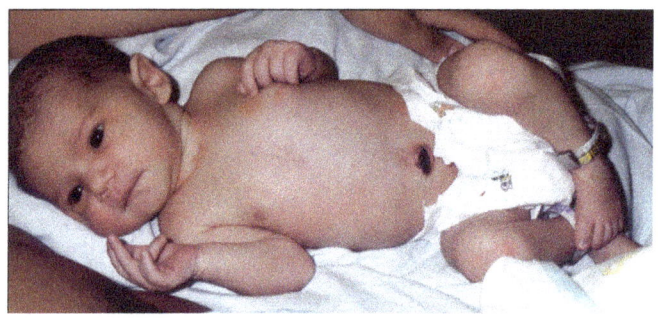

was going into distress. He declared, "We have to get this baby out now!"

Within seven minutes, we were in the hospital operating room, a C-section was completed and a healthy baby girl was born, saved from nearly dying before her life could get started.

We named her Isabel Rupa, (in Hebrew, it is Yisraela Nava) after my grandmother, Isabel. Her name means My God is Abundance, and Rupa is the Hindi word for Beautiful (Nava is the Hebrew word for Beautiful, as well).

We almost lost our first child during birth, but we are both grateful for the advanced knowledge, modern medicine and techniques that allowed her to be with us today.

5
Make It a Date

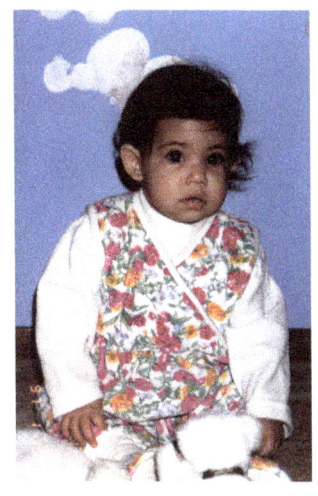

It was later in 1996. We were enjoying being parents to a newborn baby girl. After the first three months of hell, our daughter had started to sleep through the night. My wife could not believe how great it was to sleep more than three hours at a time now.

But work was busy. Running my own practice/small business was hard. Stress levels were high. And postpartum depression settled in for Tina. It was difficult. She went to her doctor and came home with an envelope. She handed it to me and said, "Dr. Karen told me to give you this." It had my name on it; inside the envelope was a prescription written out for me.

On the prescription was the command "Take your wife out on a date!"

Foothills Primary Care Centre
310, 1620 - 29 Street NW, Calgary, AB T2N 4L7
Ph: 403-221-9340   Fax: 403-221-9336

Patient Name: Tina Stanleigh

Date: _____

℞

Larry to take Tina on a date!

MD's Signature: _____

Dr. C. Scotland • Dr. C. Lebeuf • Dr. L. Ellestad • Dr. L. Morrison • Dr. M. Deyholos • Dr. P. Dunham
Dr. S. Foss • Dr. A. Luft • Dr. A. Behie • Dr. K. Roberge • Dr. S. Dezfuli • Dr. E. Kelly • Dr. C. Foyle
Dr. A. Eddy • Dr. B. Reid • Dr. G. Dufresne • Dr. C. O'Reilly • Dr. H. Downes

What brilliant insight she had! It totally made sense. We needed to reconnect as a couple, separate from our child. Children will grow up and move out. After all, we didn't live with our parents anymore. Too many couples have had children, have had them grow up, move out, and have then looked at each other and said, "Who are you?" and the marriage ends. The focus was too much on their children and not on their own personal needs.

So we engaged the babysitting services of a lovely young teenager who lived across the street, and we went on a date. It was just for dinner. We were nervous leaving our little girl behind, but she was fine. We had a wonderful meal out and Tina was happy to have a nice adult conversation. We even ended up making a life-long friendship with the waiter, Ron, who served us that night. Ron's son, daughter-in-law and grandchildren are still my patients today.

The doctor's prescription was so incredibly positive, that we made a conscious decision to go out on a date regularly. We made a regular gig out of hiring that young woman, and we went out on a date every week if we could. Many times, it was just to go out for a meal, sometimes to a movie, sometimes just for a long walk, but we did it regularly. Over the years our children got used to the fact that at least once a week they would be left with someone else. It worked well; it kept the spark of our marriage alive. In 2023,Tina and I celebrated more than 29 years together. I am still in love with her.

Some people don't do the date thing, but they find a way to take holidays together instead, away from their children. For me, it was a nice idea, but I preferred the consistency of regular dates rather than the intensity of occasional connections with my wife.

So take my advice...If you have a young family (or even if you do not), make sure you go out on dates together, with your partner in life. There is a reason you fell in love with your partner. Take the time and continue making the effort to make them feel special. Let them know they are special because the people in your life are a gift.

6
Foothills Hospital Part Two

It was November 17, 2000. We had survived the Y2K change from 1999 to 2000 without the world falling apart. A beautiful, warm Indian Summer-type Fall-in-the-Prairies sunny day. After the miracle of Isabel surviving her birth and her entry into our world, a second child was now on the way four and one-half years later.

Tina was now twelve days overdue with no hint that labour was about to start. After a consultation with the obstetrician, we debated whether to induce labour or complete an elective C-section. Based on the experience of Isabel's arrival, the obstetrician stated that he was concerned that Inducement may just turn out to be a long road to a caesarean, so we decided to have an elective C-section completed. Into the operating room

(O.R.) we went, and by 7:00 PM that same day, the procedure was completed and another healthy baby girl was born.

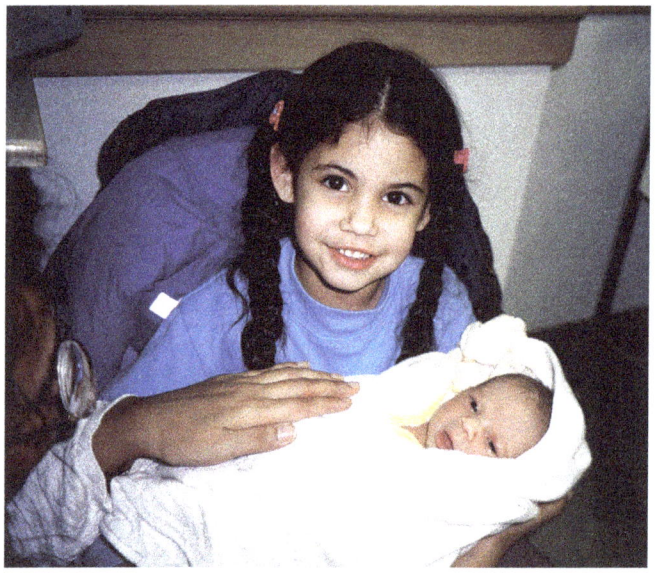

We named her Samara Rani, (the Hebrew and Hindi names are the same as her English name) after my grandfather Samuel. Her name means Guarded by God and her middle name is both the Hindi and Hebrew word for Queen.

Just minutes after the delivery, in the recovery room with family present, my beautiful, brown-skinned wife was suddenly very pale. Her sheets were soaked blood red and she was bleeding out. Tina's sister took Isabel home; I was handed our newborn daughter, Samara, and Tina was wheeled back into the O.R. Having a former staff position at the hospital, I was allowed to sit in the observation gallery, my minutes-old little girl in my arms and watched the doctors work to save Tina's life. I was confident that this was not a "big deal" and that all would be fine in short order.

After three hours in the O.R., unable to find the source of the bleeding, they suddenly stopped what they are doing. Tina's heart had gone into arrest and they had to revive her. Calm panic took over as the expert team did what they were trained to do, and they saved her.

I was sitting there, watching this unfold, holding my incredible daughter in my arms. She did not cry, did not fuss, and was perfect, just looking up at me, in the first hours after birth. This was the moment that it hit me. That Tina may not survive. Now I was frightened and scared.

I thought, "How am I going to be a father and mother to these girls without Tina?"

"What do I know about raising girls?"

"What am I going to do?..."

Fear and despair settled in.

After four hours, several pints of blood, four units of platelets and an untold amount of saline, Tina's blood had been replaced with the blood of others and her bleeding finally stopped. It was a tense three days after

that, first in the ICU, then the critical care unit and finally a regular hospital ward.

In the Book of Genesis, Chapter 28, Verse 10, there is a passage that tells the story of how Jacob lies down and places his head on a rock, falls asleep and has a dream. In his dream, he sees a ladder that ascends into Heaven. On the ladder, the Torah (or Old Testament) states that, "The Angels of God were going up and down on it." Now the great Rabbis have stated that every word in the Torah was written in the exact order as we read it. They question why that passage described the angels going up into heaven first, and not descending out of heaven. They concluded it meant that the angels have always been amongst us...they are gifts.

We almost lost our first child during her birth and with our second, we almost lost their mother. We now had healthy daughters; I had a healthy wife and we dared not risk adding to our family. A family of four was what we were blessed with, and that was what we happily accepted.

From that time forwards every year, November 17 is not just the celebration of our youngest daughter's birth, it is my own celebration of my wife's continued life and vitality, and her presence in my life. Because the people in my life are a gift.

Now, I want you to take a moment. Look at the people around you. The people you live with, the people you work with, the people who serve you. The bus drivers, the restaurant servers, the clerk at the local grocery store. They are all angels. They are all gifts.

7
Colour Blind
Part Two

We were now the proud parents of two lovely daughters and we are on a summer holiday visiting my family in Toronto. With the 4 of us, it is hard to stay with our family, so we rented a condo on the waterfront region of Harbourfront known as Queens Quay. It was a lovely area to be and many southeast Asian families were renting condos in the same building as us.

On one of our jaunts, we were riding in the glass elevator in our building when I said to my family, "Do you realize we are probably the only white family in this building."

To which my wife and both daughters laughingly exclaimed, "Look again!"

Shakespeare's play *Othello* tells the story of a Black General of the Venetian Army. Married to a white woman, the themes of black and white and racism based on skin colour were evident even in Shakespeare's time.

In Shakespeare's *The Merchant of Venice*, the Jewish Money Lender, Shylock, when asked why he wanted a pound of flesh as payment, he stated, "If you prick us, do we not bleed?" It was Shakespeare's way of asserting that there is equality between Christians and Jews and amongst all other races of human beings.

In his 1976 album *Songs in the Key of Life*, Stevie Wonder wrote and sang a song titled *Black Man*. He had previously written a song, *Livin' For The City*, about black prejudice which is still a problem today. Now he wanted to change that message, to change his theme from anger and upset about how black people are treated to one of acceptance, tolerance, harmony and love. *Black Man* was written about his desire for worldwide interracial harmony and his criticism of racism. He uses the song to highlight the accomplishments that changed the world by various people of different skin colour and genders...black, white, brown, yellow and red.

After all these years, when it comes to people, I am still colour blind. And I am proud of that. So my message is to be skin colour blind. See the person before you, not their gender, not their skin colour but the complete essence of the individual you are with.

8
To Live For

One of the ways our extended family likes to spend time together is over meals. Tina is from a family of chefs. Gujarat is known for its vegetarian dishes. Although no one is in the restaurant business, my mother-in-law is an incredible gourmet Gujarati chef who includes East African flavourings. My mother-in-law does very few things, but she does this one thing exceptionally well. Eating food prepared by my mother-in-law is better than any restaurant I have ever eaten at.

And my father-in-law is just as notable as a chef. His prawn and goat dishes are particularly memorable.

Tina's sister is nearly her mother's equal and her four brothers also enjoy being in the kitchen. Family events are always all about the food, and we eat well (unfortunately for my waistline).

At home, Tina amazes me regularly with her culinary talents. She makes delicious, healthy, tasty meals from scratch.

Why do I admire it so much? Because I hate being in the kitchen. There are 1000 things I would rather do than prepare food. Food porn, also known as the Food Channel, is often on my home TV as my wife and daughters watch it regularly.

But when it's my turn to cook, we go out or we order in. My favourite thing to make for dinner is a reservation. My favourite way to call my family to dinner is "Okay kids, get in the car!"

So, our girls are great at eating out. They have been doing so regularly since they were little children.

My profession has been good to me and I have had the good fortune to travel extensively. We have taken our daughters with us on most of our trips. As a result, we often eat out, especially when we are away.

As an aside, I have to tell you that Calgary, the city I live in, is one of the world's best kept secrets for dining. We have outstanding restaurants, with amazingly creative chefs who prepare delicious food.

And we regularly discover a dish, or a flavour, or something that is beyond compare. You know the expression, "This is so good, it is to die for?"

Well, our daughter Samara, when she was at the wise old age of about six, took exception to that. She said, "Well that is stupid! Why would you want to die? Once you are dead, you cannot enjoy it. You should say, 'It is to live for!'"

What a profound idea. She was absolutely correct. Now, we don't use the 'die for' expression. We use the expression that something is so great that it is to *live* for! And I hope you will use that too.

And this concludes this little book.

I look at my family, my team, my patients and the people I encounter every day, as the gifts they are meant to be.

I hope you take to heart my clear messages to remember why you fell in love with your partner and take the time to stay connected to them and continue to make them feel special, live your life amongst others and be skin colour blind. I also hope you keep in mind that The People In Your Life are a Gift and "great things are to live for."

POSTSCRIPT

I have enjoyed giving this complete presentation orally to many different audiences around the world. I thought my message about being skin colour blind was profoundly positive, but in these polarizing times, some people under the age of 30 are quite sensitive about a great many things.

One young black woman who attended one of my talks said this (spelling and grammatical errors were corrected from the original text)...

Hello, I really enjoyed your talk. It was very uplifting and engaging. I especially liked how you incorporated cultural competence by highlighting equality. However, as a Black person saying that you don't see colour actually minimizes the identity of marginalized people and takes away from the struggles that exist within society. Furthermore, by saying you don't see colour it suggests that differences are seen in negative light and therefore, should be ignored, when in reality differences are what can help us learn about others around us and makes the world a more exciting and cohesive environment. Therefore, I believe it is incredibly important and incumbent upon us all not only to see colour, but to have uncomfortable conversations around the disparities that exist between white folks and BIPOC (Black, Indigenous and People of Colour). In my humble opinion, it is only from a position of privilege that one can proclaim not to see colour. It is a phrase that only serves to continue the racial inequalities that persist in society and allow for some folks to ignore the plight and oppression that so many folks of colour still continue to grapple with. Perhaps a less harmful stance to take is to acknowledge that although colour and racism is a social construct, it is one that we collectively must address in a vigilant, relentless and brave manner. This requires us to reflect and examine on our own social positions and how that may unconsciously be adding on to the oppression and racism we find in all systems of society. We can begin to have honest and robust conversations with folks that don't look like us and to learn from their lived experiences. This in turn, will allow for more fruitful and deep discussions around how we frame conversations about colour and it's underpinnings of racism and perhaps advance agendas that are more inclusive, diverse and seek equality for all. I am still learning about cultural competence myself and still have a long way to go. Overall, I thought your story was very inspiring and I found myself at the edge of my seat and filled with emotions, especially when you talked about the birth of your second child and your wife's medical emergency. I hope my feedback is perceived as helpful and not discouraging. You have a gift that you should continue to share with the world.

I think that she has some valid points. As a member of the Jewish Faith, I am what is commonly known as an invisible minority. But members of the BIPOC community do not recognize that I have experienced prejudice firsthand as well, many times from members of the BIPOC community as well.

And now, in our polarizing world, even those from Central and South America of white European origin, living in Latin America, refer to themselves as people of colour as well. What that means is that more than 80% of the population of our planet belongs to the BIPOC community.

I still prefer the vision of Gene Roddenberry when he created Star Trek. He created the concept of IDIC; Infinite Diversity in Infinite Combinations. In humankind's future Star Trek Universe, skin colour was not an issue. Nor was gender, faith and other cultural items that divide us. We are all created equally and therefore, are all given equal opportunities. This is the vision I wish to embrace and therefore, will not change the message in this book. However, I thought it would be useful to add this postscript so that you, the reader, can give the topic some thought as we all move to build a better world.

About the Author

Born in Toronto, Dr. Larry Stanleigh was moved to Calgary with the Canadian Forces in 1987 and stayed.

As a keynote speaker and lecturer, he wants to create smiles and change lives through the power of storytelling and humour.

He has taken over 38 years of small business experience to speak at conferences and meetings to dentists and their teams, other healthcare groups and small businesses all over the world, helping them implement systems that are simple, intuitive and inexpensive, and which result in happier, more productive, profitable places to be, because 'Success is All About Relationships'.

Dr. Larry has written more than 80 blog articles for the Academy of General Dentistry, winning the 2015 Apex Award For Social Media Blogging, an international honour. You can read most of these articles on his speaking website www.drlarryspeaks.com

As a result of his work, relationships are developed and deepened, marketing is more effective, treatment plans are accepted, sales grow, work transforms and people's lives improve.

Dr. Larry is a GP dentist, has earned and been honoured with five fellowships, obtained an International Certificate as an Independent Medical Examiner, is also an Orofacial Pain/TMJ Dysfunction Consultant, Chief Technology Officer of Agility Guard, a Canadian Sport Performance Mouthguard company, writer/blogger, stand-up comedian, experienced master of ceremonies (MC) for charitable and entertainment events, voice actor in *No Shirt, No Shoes, Pants Optional* comedy podcast (www.pantsoptional.ca), producer of *USNA: The United States of North America* graphic novel project (www.usna.ca), and is the lead sponsor of the *Stanleigh Cup*, the Loose Moose Theatre Company's Annual High School Theatre Sports championship.

On a personal note, he is married to Tina, is inspired by his daughters, Isabel and Samara, and likes to blow the Shofar. He is also a big science fiction fan, especially the storytelling in *Star Trek*, *Star Wars* and *Babylon 5*.

This is the second edition of *The People in Your Life Are a Gift*, Dr. Larry's first book.

For more information, check him out on his Facebook Page, LinkedIn profile or his website at www.drlarryspeaks.ca.

Acknowledgements

I want to take this opportunity to thank Denise Summers of Amphora Communications (www.amphoracommunications.ca) and Cecilia Humphrey of Creative Capture (www.creativecapture.ca) for their invaluable assistance and expertise in helping me make this book a real thing, and no longer just something in my head.

I also want to thank my brother, Allan Stanleigh (www.usna.ca) and Will Ferguson (www.willferguson.ca) for their assistance in copy editing, proofreading and overall encouragement.

> The past is history.
> The future is a mystery.
> Today is a Gift.
> That is why they call it The Present.

www.ingramcontent.com/pod-product-compliance
Lightning Source LLC
Chambersburg PA
CBHW042131100526
44587CB00026B/4252